An opinionated guide to

LONDON PLAYGROUNDS

Written by
EMMY WATTS

Hazel (left) aged 3, with Olive, aged 5, Victoria Park Playgrounds (no.32)

GO OUT AND LET THEM GO WILD

Permanent markers on the wall. Ketchup on the window. Credit cards pushed through the cracks of the floorboards. Having a family in London teaches you that if you don't find a playground outside, they'll find one at home.

Fortunately, despite the concrete and congestion, London not only has great parks but utterly fabulous outdoor play spaces, too. These brightly coloured pressure-release valves serve both as a destination and a passing panacea. The trouble is knowing which of the thousands on offer are actually worth visiting.

Thankfully, Emmy, our brilliant writer, has made the decision for you (as we know you have neither the time or energy to make any more decisions in life). This is the book we longed for when we first had our kids and wanted them to swing on some monkey bars rather than play on our frayed patience.

Martin & Ann (with Olive & Hazel)
Hoxton Mini Press

Royal Air Force Museum Playground (no.9)
Opposite: Spring Park Playground (no.15)

Claremont Park Playground (no.12)

Discover Children's Story Centre (no.35)
Opposite: Tumbling Bay Playground (no.31)

THE POWER OF PLAY(GROUNDS)

Playgrounds are the unifying backdrops to our childhoods. If we were all asked to jot down three playground memories, they'd probably be roughly comparable. Who could forget the chlorinated whiff of a freshly filled paddling pool, or the thrill of a big kid pushing us too fast on the roundabout? We'd recall the ecstasy of stumbling across an incredible new one. The comfort of an old faithful. The friends we made. The scars we earned.

In a world that isn't built for children, playgrounds provide havens for them to collaborate and experiment, places where they are allowed to simply be young. In London, where the population of under-16s is nearly two million but living space is at a premium and decent-sized gardens are practically mythical, playgrounds offer an indispensable public good.

London is home to a dizzying number of playgrounds, some positively spectacular and some admittedly less so. I've spent the last eight years seeking out the best playgrounds from across the capital, while my kids have been given the incredibly tough job of testing them out. And while you might assume we'd found the formula for the perfect playground somewhere along the way, we haven't.

Even the designers seem to be scratching their heads when it comes to what makes the ultimate play space. Maybe that's because there's simply no such thing. Take Elephant Park's gorgeously landscaped splash pool (no.38) – by no means an exhaustive playground but an incredible setting for a summer's day. Or Muf's concrete-slabbed Golden Lane Estate Play Space (no.3) – tiny, but with inventive features that make it the perfect way to kill 30 minutes in the City. Maybe variety is the very thing kids need.

And what about us grown-ups? Surely we need variety, too? We spend such a large chunk of our lives in these places, we might as well enjoy a change of scenery while we're there.

Then there's the endless bribery potential. Your offspring might not give a hoot about that new art exhibition you want to see on the other side of town, but the promise of swinging by a great playground afterwards might be all the motivation they require.

Some of these spaces are simply so great they must be seen to be believed. With the exception of a couple of ancient slides, most are a million miles more impressive than anything the vast majority of us will have experienced in our youths, which might be profoundly unjust, but at least we can enjoy them vicariously through our kids. In fact, never mind vicariously. I'll see you on the zip wire.

Emmy Watts
London, 2025

Emmy Watts is a London-based writer and kids' activity blogger. She's authored 15 books for Hoxton Mini Press, including two *Opinionated Guides* to navigating London with children. She can usually be found scouting out new playgrounds with her two young daughters.

BEST FOR...

Grand days out

Hampton Court's Magic Garden (no.43) is practically a full day out on its own. Add in a romp through the palace and meander through the maze, and you've got an epic adventure. Or head to Hobbledown Heath (no.55), a mystical land of enchanting animals and imaginative outdoor playscapes.

Meeting non-parent friends

Highgate Wood's (no.13) scenic location and nearby cafe make it the perfect spot for child-free mates and chill-free little monsters. Or grab a couple of coffees from one of Exmouth Market's many stylish cafes and head to Spa Fields' (no.4) picturesque play area for a catch-up while they frolic.

Adventurous big kids

With its perplexing labyrinths and towering timber structures, Three Corners (no.1) is a dream come true for older ones. Or try Cator Park North (no.42), whose lofty nests and twisting tube slides mean it's not for the fainthearted.

Mixed ages

It's rare to find a playground that caters to toddlers through to teens, but Paddington Recreation Ground (no.54) is the ultimate example, with two beautifully designed spaces connected via a bridge. Or head to Coram's Fields (no.5), a kids-only park with enough play areas to keep everyone happy.

Tiny toddlers

Harbour Quay's (no.27) pint-sized playground is ideal for under-5s, with its low-walled labyrinth and sensory features. Meanwhile, in Bloomsbury, Alf Barrett Playground (no.2) offers loads for little ones, from baby swings to gentle clambering, all reassuringly encircled by a toddler-proof gate.

Design-conscious carers

When you spend such a large chunk of your life in playgrounds, you might as well pick one that's aesthetically pleasing. The Golden Lane Estate's (no.3) architect-designed play space fits the bill, with its muted palette and multilevel concrete rockery, while the Clapham Park Estate's (no.49) spiralling 1960s slide structure is a must-visit for Brutalism buffs.

Sweltering summers

When the temperature rises, head to one of the capital's revitalising splash pads to cool down. Favourites include Elephant Springs' (no.38) natural waterscape play area, Victoria Park's (no.32) spiralling concrete splash pool and Tumbling Bay's (no.31) enticing dams, streams and water pumps.

Accessibility

Gloucester Gate's playground (no.8) was designed with inclusivity in mind, with a wheelchair-accessible roundabout and ramp, plus raised tables for water play. Similarly, Greenwich Park Playground (no.40) was devised with input from parents of disabled children, and features a widened slide, thoughtfully placed paths and plenty of sensory elements.

CENTRAL

1
THREE CORNERS ADVENTURE PLAYGROUND

Impressive space with surprising features

Three Corners is everything you could want in an adventure playground, offering a play experience like you've never seen before – that is, unless you've previously encountered a vertical labyrinth spun from red netting, or a mirror maze housed in a towering timber castle. There are more traditional features, from a curly tube slide to a zip wire, but this is still far from your average playtime. Families with under-6s get just two hours a week to get their Three Corners fix, though with such vertiginous structures it's really better suited to older kids, who can be dropped off for a longer play while you indulge in an idle mooch around the cool cafes and boutiques of neighbouring Exmouth Market.

Northampton Road, EC1R 0HU
Nearest station: Farringdon
Facilities: Toilets

2
ALF BARRETT PLAYGROUND

Central spot with playful design

Once one of the saddest spots in central London, this shady pocket park underwent a magical transformation in 2022 that saw its tired metal structures traded in for an inventive fairytale playscape helmed by a gigantic lizard. Aimed at under-8s, the playground might be small, but its design offers virtually limitless potential, with rolling hills to scale, stepping stones to navigate and an elevated platform to occupy. Devised to be more inclusive than its predecessor, the playground also boasts a wheelchair-friendly layout, complete with accessible roundabout and wide slide. Combine with a visit to eccentric gaming arcade Novelty Automation or buzzy bowling alley All Star Lanes.

32 Old Gloucester Street, WC1N 3AD
Nearest station: Holborn

CENTRAL

3
GOLDEN LANE ESTATE PLAY SPACE

Pocket estate playground

It's technically reserved for the young residents of Chamberlin, Powell and Bon's Grade II-listed estate, but it's hard to resist a romp around this small but perfectly formed play space. Designed with imaginative input from local schoolkids, this sunken site might be hard to locate, but it's a delight once you do, with inventive multifunctional play furniture and a soothing neutral aesthetic that might make hanging out here a lengthier affair than you'd imagine. A tiny stage, retro-style climbing frame and even a secret slide have all been cunningly crammed into this elliptical plot, while its tightly stacked slabs of natural stone offer boundless bouldering opportunities. Stop off en route to the Barbican for family films and conservatory capers.

Golden Lane, EC1Y 0RD
Nearest station: Barbican

CENTRAL

4
SPA FIELDS PLAYGROUND

Fantasy playscape dreamt up by kids

Aliens exist. At least, that's what this otherworldly playground might have you believe. Here, strange UFO-like structures rest on a carpet of mysterious mounds, as if ready to take off. Believe it or not, its design is not the work of extra-terrestrials, but a bunch of local schoolkids hankering for a fantastical, age-inclusive place to meet and play. In this imagined world, tightropes bridge gaping hollows, wonky steps pave the way up to spike-topped forts and chairs perch atop 6-foot ladders like the thrones of leggy overlords. Such a non-prescriptive design makes this the ultimate backdrop for imaginative play – and there's plenty more room for that at the nearby Postal Museum, whose themed play space is role-play heaven for 0–8s.

Skinner Street, EC1R 0WX
Nearest stations: Angel, Farringdon
Facilities: Toilets, picnic benches

CENTRAL

5
CORAM'S FIELDS

Historic kids-only park

Its playgrounds might not be anything particularly pioneering, but Coram's Fields has been a trailblazer for children's rights for nearly three centuries. Established as London's first public playground in 1936, the 12-acre park was once the site of philanthropist Thomas Coram's Foundling Hospital for abandoned children and remains the only green space in London to refuse entry to adults who aren't accompanied by a child. Equipment ranges from toddler-ready sand-play structures in primary hues to a majestic treehouse tower and climbing wall for big kids, with wooden multi-play structures bridging the gap between the two. Come via the neighbouring Foundling Museum, whose exhibits tell the heartrending story of the former hospital in a child-friendly way.

93 Guildford Street, WC1N 1DN
Nearest station: Russell Square
Facilities: Toilets, cafe, picnic benches

NORTH

6
STATIONERS PARK

Towers and teepees in award-winning space

With its ramshackle aesthetic, all Tolkienesque turrets and stilted walkways, this small but well-loved park's fairytale fortress is one of north London's most easily recognisable climbing frames, boasting rickety bridges, treacherous entry points and snaking slides that make for some refreshingly risky play. Alongside timber teepees and tyre swings, there's also a gentler (though still extremely popular) play area that's perfect for under-5s. Here, smaller explorers can navigate everything from Wendy houses to ever-present bouncers. Start your visit at the cafe kiosk on the park's north side, where you can fuel up on chocolate banana bread before hitting the swings, then head home via local treasure Niddle Noddle for toys, kidswear and a ride on the in-store helter-skelter.

Mayfield Road, N8 9LP
Nearest station: Harringay
Facilities: Cafe, picnic benches

7
ALEXANDRA ROAD PARK

Inventive playground on a Brutalist estate

Originally constructed for the young residents of the surrounding Alexandra and Ainsworth estate – a Brutalist masterpiece that's served as the backdrop to many a noirish TV show – this quirky playground underwent an award-winning revamp in 2015 that combines elements of the original design with modern equipment. Arranged across three walled outdoor 'rooms', the one-of-a-kind space comprises a striking red swing area, a spectacular yellow climbing frame recommended for ages 6+ and a more traditional, though still pleasingly odd, wood-dominated playground for under-5s. Once they're all played out, head to Abbey Road to recreate The Beatles' iconic album cover. Or try the Sherriff Centre for soft play and good hot chocolate.

Langtry Walk, NW8 0DU
Nearest station: South Hampstead

NORTH

8
GLOUCESTER GATE PLAYGROUND

Natural playscape in Regent's Park

Regent's Park's most northerly playground was renovated in 2020, when a rather stark 1980s arrangement of turreted slides and retro roundabouts was magicked into a dreamily landscaped natural play area. Designed as an inclusive space with meandering wheelchair-ready ramps and accessible swings and roundabouts, the new Gloucester Gate is wildly popular with local (and not-so-local) kids all year round, bridging age brackets as much as it does abilities with its teen-gratifying zip wire and toddler-pleasing sand- and water-play area. Head here in good weather with buckets and spades, and in bad with wellies and puddle suits – or just swing by on your way home from neighbouring London Zoo.

11 Gloucester Gate, NW1 4HG
Nearest station: Camden Town
Facilities: Toilets, baby change, cafe, picnic benches

NORTH

9
ROYAL AIR FORCE MUSEUM PLAYGROUND

Aircraft-themed play space on museum grounds

Young aviation fans will be flying high when they spy this themed playground, which draws inspiration from the RAF Museum's vast assortment of military aircraft. What the space lacks in square footage, it makes up for with its generous array of unique apparatus, including a hovering yellow rescue helicopter for clambering, a double Concorde slide and replica Spitfire, plus a scaled-down version of the site's watchtower that's perfect for hide and seek. Access the playground via the seriously underrated main museum, which spans six literal hangars (it occupies the site of the former Hendon Aerodrome) stuffed with characterful aircraft and engaging interactives.

Grahame Park Way, NW9 5LL
Nearest station: Colindale
Facilities: Toilets, baby change, cafe, picnic benches

NORTH

10
KILBURN GRANGE PARK PLAY AREA

Nature-inspired playscape in a former arboretum

Rising from the ashes of the adventure playground that once occupied this leafy site, this adventurous children's playground might lack playworkers and loose parts, but it certainly lives up to its name, offering 0–14s the chance to boldly play in a way that many more prescriptive playgrounds don't allow. The main event is a stunning yet seemingly haphazard arrangement of logs that references the site's former life as a Victorian arboretum, with its nest-like hideaways, treetop tunnels and high-speed slide. Elsewhere, find water play, a standing seesaw and long-chained swings that make for a seriously thrilling ride. Should the weather take a turn, seek sanctuary in the Sherriff Centre's three-storey soft play and cafe – all housed in a Victorian church.

Messina Avenue, NW6 4LD
Nearest station: Brondesbury

11
MARYLEBONE GREEN PLAYGROUND

Popular playground with arty attitude

Unlike neighbouring Gloucester Gate (no.8), which seems to blend effortlessly into Regent's Park's natural environs, this unusual playground, with an imposing concrete folly as its centrepiece, feels at odds with its surroundings – namely the park's manicured English Gardens. There's a good reason for that, though: the folly's design draws inspiration from Frieze, the illustrious art fair that pops up in the park every year and is no stranger to outlandish structures. Perched on the edge of a huge sandpit and water-play area, it houses a large slide, climbing wall and 'secret' room equipped with a large xylophone, while the more usual suspects (roundabouts, swings) are sited close by. Head here during Frieze Sculpture season for an added dose of culture.

The Regent's Park, Chester Road, NW1 4NR
Nearest station: Regent's Park
Facilities: Toilets, baby change, cafe, picnic benches

NORTH

12

CLAREMONT PARK PLAYGROUND

Inclusive playscape in biodiverse surrounds

It might be inelegantly sandwiched between motorways and railway lines, but that doesn't make this capacious playground any less impressive. Designed for all ages and abilities, this surprisingly peaceful playscape boasts wheelchair-accessible surfaces and apparatus; sensory elements including musical instruments and diverse textures; and equipment to challenge even long-legged teens. Clever landscaping ups the enjoyment factor, with stone climbing walls, a natural water-play area, and a strong visual cohesion with the wider park, whose varied plant life promotes biodiversity. The presence of an on-site food and drink kiosk – along with outposts of Jewish bakery Karma Bread and Neapolitan pizzeria Happy Face – make staying all day a real possibility.

Claremont Way, NW2 1AJ
Nearest station: Brent Cross West
Facilities: Toilets, baby change, cafe, picnic benches

13
HIGHGATE WOOD PLAYGROUND

Retro fun in an ancient forest

Its equipment may be as antiquated as the surrounding woodland (or, at least, it seems that way), but that doesn't make this iconic playground any less worth a visit. In fact, its nostalgic delights are all part of the quirky charm, with fan favourites including wobbly 1990s ride-on vehicles, a step-mounted tunnel slide and copious climbing frames. Head here after your Sunday stroll, scheduling a stop at the Grocery Post for coffee, pastries and a bottle of organic wine for later, then sate their post-playground appetites with kids' comfort classics from the neighbouring Pavilion Cafe, run by falafel aficionados Hoxton Beach.

Muswell Hill Road, N10 3JN
Nearest station: Highgate
Facilities: Toilets, baby change, cafe, picnic benches

14
ASTEY'S ROW PLAYGROUND

Islington's rainbow-hued boulderscape

London's most colourful playground is also probably its narrowest, occupying a curious, snake-shaped plot behind Essex Road station that was once a 17th-century waterway. The playground's awkward shape has no bearing on its fun factor, however, with an interesting array of apparatus – both conventional and more imaginative – on offer. Older kids are well catered for, courtesy of a wobbly-rope climbing frame, balance-log assault course and a pair of somewhat precarious slides, while younger ones will appreciate the water pump-equipped sandpit and highlighter-bright boulders. Load up on coffee and croissants from Popham's en route, and don't miss indie kids' boutique Molly Meg for dreamy homeware and gifts.

Canonbury Villas, N1 2HE
Nearest station: Essex Road

15
SPRING PARK PLAYGROUND

Natural playscape overlooking wetlands

Perched on the edge of the picturesque Woodberry Wetlands and serene New River Walk, this charming playground offers the ideal stop-off for scenic family strolls, as well as boasting one of the capital's most spectacular playground backdrops – something that's more important than you'd think. Equipment varies from a toddler-ready multi-play frame to a lofty pyramid tower that bigger kids can launch themselves from by way of a gargantuan tube slide, as well as a climbing wall and multiple balance apparatus. Best of all, the playable space is massive, spanning acres of beautifully landscaped terrain with not a single car in sight. Climbing wall whet their appetite? Give them a real challenge at the nearby Castle Climbing Centre.

6 Town Court Path, Woodberry Down, N4 2TJ
Nearest station: Manor House
Facilities: Cafe

NORTH

16

HIGHBURY FIELDS PLAYGROUND

Expansive playscape with original mound slide

If ever a playground had it all, it's this eclectic gem in Islington's largest park, whose exhilarating patchwork of diverse equipment spans an enormous sandpit scattered with toddler equipment, a stimulating big kids' zone with towering pyramids, a soaring zip wire and a flame-hued wooden climber. Meanwhile, well-loved – but still fully functional – retro apparatus includes an excellent pedal-powered roundabout and one of the best examples of a mound slide you'll likely ever encounter, and the small but welcome splash pad is a powerful kid magnet come summer. Come armed with a large matcha latte from Kissa Wa Cafe, an off-the-beaten-track Japanese on the adjacent Corsica Street.

8 Highbury Crescent, N5 1RN
Nearest station: Highbury & Islington
Facilities: Toilets, cafe, picnic benches

17
BARNARD ADVENTURE PLAYGROUND

Charismatic space with classic design

With sweeping walkways and towering treetop dens that will scare the living daylights out of even the most permissive parents, this sprawling playground on stilts is definitely not for the fainthearted, but confident climbers will adore it. Speeding zip wires, a large climbing wall and an amphitheatre where kids can stage plays or whoosh down a ramp on battered ride-ons are just some of the treats that lie in store for young visitors. Like all adventure playgrounds in the borough, Barnard limits its open-access hours for families to 11:30am–1:30pm on a Saturday, but this should be more than enough time to tire out tinies. Afterwards, head to Angel's Polka Theatre for inspiring puppetry for kids of all ages.

Copenhagen Street, N1 0FB
Nearest station: Angel
Facilities: Toilets

NORTH

18
HORNSEY PARK PLAYGROUND

Compact site with creative structures

Built to serve the residents of Haringey's Clarendon Gasworks development, this small but interesting spot has filled a void in the area's play provision, expanding its appeal far beyond the estate's edge. Where many playground designs feel chaotic, this feels considered, with equipment limited to three key structures, each offering endless scope. A honeycomb-like arrangement of den structures caters to smaller explorers, while a sprawling concrete rope course accommodates bigger kids. A lofty octagonal tower commands a hillside position that allows for an extra-long slide and a thrilling ride back down to earth. Post-play, head to the Goodness Brewing Company for pints, pizza and weekend bouncy-castle joy.

Hornsey Park Road, N8 0JX
Nearest stations: Hornsey, Turnpike Lane

NORTH

19
SOMERFORD GROVE PLAYGROUND

Colourful, community-focused space

Tucked discreetly in the shadow of Spurs' Stadium and mostly populated by the local kids who helped build it, this magical space oozes community spirit without ever feeling exclusive. On Saturdays, it opens its doors to children of all ages, albeit with grown-ups required to accompany under-6s for the duration, while its after-school provision for older kids includes a weekly girls-only session. Vibrant greenhouses perch atop mature trees, an elliptical den offers shelter as well as climbing opportunities thanks to a well-placed platform and a multi-storey tower provides endless scope for clambering and (cushioned) jumping. Supposing that's not enough exertion for one day, Roller Nation runs a relaxed Family Jam roller disco every weekend.

Park Lane Close, N17 0HL
Nearest station: Northumberland Park
Facilities: Toilets

NORTH

20
QUEEN'S PARK PLAYGROUND

Verdant space with city farm

While not groundbreaking as far as its equipment goes, Queen's Park offers a pretty excellent playground by most kids' standards. Large and leafy, this popular spot will challenge adventurers of all ages with its looming pyramid slide, giant log jumble and rocketing zip wire; while its well-secured under-5s zone invites little ones to explore a sandy settlement of charmingly retro playhouses and vehicles. Surprisingly few people seem to be aware of the tiny children's farm on the other side of the park, but the paddling pool commands a great deal of attention come the summer months, while nearby Yogaloft's oddly serene soft play boasts comfy sofas and an excellent vegetarian cafe.

Kingswood Avenue, NW6 6EN
Nearest station: Queen's Park
Facilities: Toilets, baby change, cafe, picnic benches

21
ST JUDE STREET GARDEN

Unique timber-pole playscape

Whether they're navigating the masts of a vast pirate ship, bounding through the treetops of a magical forest or leapfrogging podiums to evade a terrible lava monster below, kids of all ages will reap endless joy from this distinctive timber-pole-studded playscape. Redesigned in 2025 with input from local schoolkids, this once-underused playground now takes full advantage of its sizeable, if narrow, plot, with distinct infant and junior structures whose forms mirror the other and blend climbing nets, balance ropes, thrilling slides and crows' nests among the vertical poles. When their bodies are weary, head to Draughts board game cafe for a more cerebral challenge – or just a plate of nachos and some Snakes & Ladders.

St Jude Street, N16 8JT
Nearest station: Dalston Kingsland

22
HOPPA PLAY AND SKATE PARK

Destination playground for high-energy fun

Hoppa, both a Swedish word meaning 'to hop or jump' and a Dutch exclamation of encouragement or excitement, is a fitting designation for this electrifying playground. Located at the heart of Edmonton's new Meridian Water development, the much-needed recreational space was designed with local primary school children to serve the entire community, with wheelchair access throughout and challenging equipment and skate facilities for all ages. Smaller children can commandeer tiny teepees and beat balance trails while the big ones conquer twin towers linked via a treacherous rope tunnel, before joining forces at the water-play area. When they're finished at Hoppa, why not hop over to AirHop, Enfield's breathtaking adventure trampoline park, for more high-octane fun?

Vetchling Way, N18 2FR
Nearest station: Meridian Water

EAST

23
PARSLOES PARK

Vibrant artist-designed playscape

It's not often councils commission artists to design their playgrounds – and when they do, the resulting spaces are usually criticised for prioritising style over play value. While that might be the case for at least one of this Dagenham park's eye-catching playgrounds, it's hard to refute the joy of their colour palettes or the quirkiness of their forms. Eva Rothschild's Parsloes Memphis is a dream for leggy older kids and teens with its brightly hued steel pyramids, while Yinka Ilori's Flamboyance of Flamingos will delight younger tots with its colourful flamingo bouncers and nest-shaped slide. Investigate them on the way to Barking Sportshouse and Gym – home to a massive trampoline park and soft play that kids will lose their minds over.

Ivy Walk, RM9 5RX
Nearest station: Becontree

EAST

24
WEST HAM PARK PLAYGROUND

Themed space with explorer's ship and swings

In 2022, this leafy park's tired but well-loved playground underwent its biggest revamp in 35 years, a move that saw its mismatched patchwork of faded metal apparatus replaced by a more cohesive scheme themed around the park's botanical history. Invitingly scalable organic play sculptures, including an interpretation of former landowner John Fothergill's Explorer Ship, extensive water features and an abundance of sustainable timber and stone make the new design a much more attractive play prospect for kids – not to mention a more inviting backdrop for their adults. Don't miss the site's most treasured possession – a pair of retro monkey swings that, despite losing their swing function, retain every ounce of their 1980s charm.

Upton Lane, E7 9PU
Nearest station: Plaistow
Facilities: Toilets, cafe, picnic benches

25
BIODIVERSITY PLAYGROUND

Pond-themed play from Danish master

Danish playground designer Monstrum has successfully created one of the capital's most magnificent playscapes on what might otherwise have been a rather uninspiring site, wedged between a mainline rail station and a shopping mall. Drawing inspiration from the work of folklore master Hans Christian Andersen, this magical play area is notable for its imaginative themed structures – all beautifully constructed using sustainable timber. Bubblegum-pink lily-pad bouncers, sloping white origami boats, ornamental bridges, a leaf-green frog slide and an enormous flame-hued koi carp float on a sea of blue and green spongy surfacing, offering a welcome break from the monotony of traditional playground design – not to mention the madness of Westfield on a weekend.

Westfield Stratford City, E20 1EJ
Nearest station: Stratford
Facilities: Toilets, baby change, cafe

EAST

26
SUNRISE CLOSE PLAY AREA

Design-conscious playscape for all ages

Amsterdam-based architects Carve designed this unique East Village playscape to mimic the triangular geometry of the surrounding apartment blocks. Children of all ages are well catered for, with both big and little kids' areas separated by spurting play fountains that will be popular with both. On the under-5s side, tangerine-hued pods conceal tiny swings, rope ladders and hidden slides. For older ones, a large cluster of modular play crystals forms a maze suspended on stilts, providing infinite possibilities as well as a pleasing visual contrast in a rich shade of grey-blue. Neighbouring Bakehouse by Signorelli is ideal for a post-play refuel and also runs popular Little Bakers sessions, offering younger kids the chance to decorate their own cupcakes over a babyccino.

Sunrise Close, E20 1DU
Nearest station: Stratford

27
HARBOUR QUAY MAZE PLAY AREA

Sensory fun for younger kids

While not a 'destination' playground, this small but sweet quayside diversion is the ideal place to deposit grotty toddlers, who'll lap up its arrangement of lilliputian bridges, perplexing paths and tiny tunnels while their grown-ups admire the river view. The site might be pint-sized, but the magical mirror-maze design makes it feel significantly bigger, while sensory elements including musical instruments, talking tubes and tactile installations will keep little ones entertained. Still not satisfied? Check out neighbouring Harbord Square Park's equally diminutive under-5s play area for sand and water fun, featuring easy-to-push pumps and a dam system designed to encourage collaborative play. Alternatively, visit London Museum Docklands to explore their interactive Mudlarks gallery.

Park Drive, E14 5FW
Nearest station: Canary Wharf

28
ALL MEAD GARDENS

Estate playground with concrete sculptures

A fishy surprise awaits curious kids at Hackney's Kingsmead Estate. Tucked between the red-brick blocks, the beloved 'Fish Playground' is nicknamed for the huge concrete fish head that forms its unlikely centrepiece, functioning as a clubhouse and rain shelter, among countless other possibilities. Directly opposite, what could feasibly be London's most precarious slide – accessed via a long ladder and completely uncovered despite its elevation and sharp twists and turns – adds to All Mead's list of oddities. Next door in the under-5s playground things are equally unconventional, with fish-shaped bouncers and stone sculptures orbited by colourful tarmac, and a network of peekaboo-perfect wooden walls. A must for post-Chats Palace frolics.

Kingsmead Estate, E9 5QN
Nearest station: Homerton

EAST

29

FORRESTER WAY PLAY AREA

Pocket park with mammoth play tower

Stratford is home to an unholy number of playgrounds thanks to a policy that requires every housing development built in the wake of the 2012 Olympic Games to have one. While the lucky young residents of E15 and E20 have around a dozen to choose from, most kids would be overjoyed just to live close to this epic play tower, whose breathtaking tunnel slide more than justifies a vertiginous scramble through several layers of net to reach it. Once the site of an Olympic parking lot, this pond-encircled plot is blissfully calm – save for the excited shrieks of children whizzing down that slide – and makes for a great post-shop stop-off, far from the clamour of Westfield.

Forrester Way, E15 1GH
Nearest station: Stratford

EAST

30
BARKING PARK PLAYGROUND

Sand, sailing and summertime splashing

If ever a green space was made for summer, it's this tranquil Victorian park. Home to a popular splash pad that opens from May, and a boating lake where families can rent unicorn-shaped pedalos, the park also hosts an enticingly sandy playground whose equipment appears to be sinking into the golden depths. While the latter is open year-round, it's best enjoyed when the sun's out and the neighbouring cafe does a roaring trade in iced coffees and ice creams in a mind-boggling array of flavours. Equipment is particularly suited to tots, who'll delight in investigating the three-piece shipwreck, exploring the Wendy house village and wriggling through the red hillside tunnel. Head here from late spring with buckets and spades.

Longbridge Road, IG11 8TA
Nearest station: Barking
Facilities: Toilets, baby change, cafe, picnic benches

31
TUMBLING BAY PLAYGROUND

Natural play paradise in the Olympic Park

Forget Anish Kapoor's *Orbit*; this sprawling utopia is arguably the 2012 Olympic Games' greatest legacy, beloved by children across the capital and headlining many a tiny tourist's 'to do' list. Here, on the northern edge of the Queen Elizabeth Olympic Park, intrepid little explorers can scale nest-like climbing structures, tackle web-like rope canopies, cross rickety bridges and explore an elaborate system of dams and splash pools. There's plenty to entertain all ages for hours – and the adjacent cafe will facilitate as many snack, toilet and coffee breaks as you desire – but there's stacks more to explore in the wider park, from the inspiring London Aquatics Centre to the shiny new V&A East Storehouse.

Olympic Park Avenue, E20 1DY
Nearest station: Stratford
Facilities: Toilets, baby change, cafe, picnic benches

32
VICTORIA PARK PLAYGROUNDS

Fun and frolics in east London's largest park

So-called because it once hosted a speakers' corner to rival Hyde Park's, the 'People's Park' is so well geared towards its child-encumbered visitors, it may as well call itself the Parents' Park. One of Britain's oldest public commons, this family favourite possesses not one, but *two* popular playgrounds, two child-friendly cafes and a brilliant summertime splash pool. Both playgrounds have had several of their original wooden structures replaced by some profoundly ugly metal equipment, though the larger of the two still impresses with its trio of breathtaking hillside slides, a bouncy bridge sandwiched between two rope climbing pyramids and a series of musical jumping pads.

E9 5DU
Nearest station: Hackney Wick
Facilities: Toilets, baby change, cafe, picnic benches

33

STONEBRIDGE GARDENS

Popular park with serpentine play sculpture

Hop off the Windrush line and straight into the gaping maw of a 60-foot-long concrete serpent – the slithering centrepiece of Haggerston's best-loved playground. Better known locally as 'Snake Park', the recently revamped play space packs in plenty beside its decades-old play sculpture – most notably an arduous play tower whose bracing tunnel slide spits young adventurers out into a generously proportioned sandpit, complete with pulleys and buckets. Elsewhere, they'll discover a balance trail, a canopied den and copious swings, while the mosaicked snake's meandering form invites infinite scrambling. Decamp to Japanese cafe Toconoco come lunchtime for seaweed-wrapped riceballs and role-play shenanigans in the toy-stuffed kids' corner.

6 Arbutus Street, E8 4DT
Nearest station: Haggerston

34
HACKNEY DOWNS PLAYGROUND

Large play area with diverse equipment

The animal mosaics adorning its beloved shelter provided the inspiration for an upgrade to this crowd-pleasing playground, with a plethora of stone and other natural materials used to mimic wild habitats such as savannas and mountain ranges. While expanded to include teen-friendly climbing equipment, swings and playful natural elements, many of the well-loved original structures have been retained – most notably a large, ramped climbing structure, a retro metal train bench and the aforementioned shelter. Good sight lines, clean toilets and plenty of seating ups the grown-up appeal – which is just as well, since you may be here for the long haul. Arm yourself with caffeine and pastries from the resident Calma coffee van before settling in.

49 Downs Road, E5 8QP
Nearest station: Hackney Downs
Facilities: Toilets, baby change, picnic benches

35
DISCOVER CHILDREN'S STORY CENTRE

Literary attraction's folklore-inspired playground

Its three floors of immersive Story Worlds might make this treasured Stratford attraction a rainy-day failsafe, but its recently refurbished fairytale Story Garden is a draw in itself. Taking inspiration from everything from Slavic folklore to the dawn of the Space Age and Discover's resident space-monster mascot, Hootah, the garden's idiosyncratic structures encourage imaginative play while giving the sense that they could uproot themselves and fly away at any moment. The enclosed nature of the garden, which is only accessible via the centre, along with its leafy landscaping, allows children to fully immerse themselves, while carers grab a ringside seat – and a coffee from the outdoor shack on weekends and school holidays.

383–387 High Street, E15 4QZ
Nearest station: Stratford High Street
Facilities: Toilets, baby change, cafe, picnic benches

36
BRUNSWICK PARK PLAYGROUND

Bijou green space with an independent cafe

Size-wise, this four-acre green space might pale in comparison to its neighbour, the rambling Burgess Park, but don't let that deter you from dragging the gang here. For nestled among cool Camberwell's Victorian villas, you'll find one of south London's most family-friendly spaces: a leafy haven that's a parental saviour year-round thanks to its popular playground and adjoining coffee-and-cake kiosk. Both bumbling toddlers and fearless big kids are well catered for, with twin red-and-yellow wood structures (one a Wendy house, the other a more precarious construction that encourages riskier play), as well as standard equipment. Pop by on the way to South London Gallery's monthly Sunday Spot workshop for 5–12s.

148 Elmington Road, SE5 7RA
Nearest station: Denmark Hill
Facilities: Cafe, picnic benches

SOUTH

37
BURGESS PARK WOODLAND PLAYGROUND

Natural playscape with treetop dens

So-called because its towering natural play structures provide an experience akin to swinging (or fumbling) through the treetops, Burgess Park's newest playground offers a stimulating experience with the visuals to match. Built around a series of tree-like three-dimensional nests, each with ten sides, the playground invites adventurous children of all ages to crawl through rope tunnels, scramble up climbing nets, shoot down slides and battle obstacles in whatever order they please. Elsewhere, little explorers will find balance beams, stepping poles and swings for all ages and abilities, while on the park's north side, a brightly coloured tarmac playscape offers a different sensory experience (plus cooling water jets in the summer months).

40 New Church Road, SE5 7JJ
Nearest station: Oval
Facilities: Toilets, baby change, cafe, picnic benches

SOUTH

38
ELEPHANT SPRINGS

Stunning natural splash park

For the few short weeks every year when play fountains seem like the only place on Earth where you won't evaporate, Elephant Springs is parental heaven. Forming part of the recreational space that rose from the ashes of the neo-Brutalist Heygate Estate, this summer-ready spot is the Rolls-Royce of splash pads, constructed from 600 landscaped hunks of slip-resistant Italian stone that form the stage for motion-sensitive water jets, miniature waterfalls and babbling brooks, with gushing hand pumps and habitually damp slides upping the excitement. A large sandpit, swinging rope hammocks and slab seating encourage all-day loafing, while a perfectly situated coffee kiosk – and sourdough pizza from Four Hundred Rabbits – should keep everyone sated until home time.

21 Ash Avenue, Elephant Park, SE17 1FR
Nearest station: Elephant & Castle
Facilities: Toilets, baby change, cafe, picnic benches

SOUTH

39

JUBILEE GARDENS PLAYGROUND

Buzzy riverside hotspot

This permanently busy playground's popularity may be largely down to its tourist-trap location at the foot of the London Eye, but that's not to say it's not a great one anyway. Recently given a serious boost in the form of a ship-shaped structure with wonky gangways and below-deck dens, it also boasts a big-kid-friendly log assault course with colossal climbing webs, as well as cute hidey houses and static animals that cater to the opposite end of the age scale. Add in wobble boards, talking tubes and swinging boats, and you've got yourself one heck of a playground. Next stop, supposing you can drag them away: the Southbank Centre's weekly Rug Rhymes sessions or Brewdog Waterloo's massive slide.

Belvedere Road, SE1 7PG
Nearest station: Waterloo
Facilities: Toilets, baby change, cafe, picnic benches

40
GREENWICH PARK PLAYGROUND

Accessible play with nautical theme

London's most beautiful park has a rich history of recreation, having hosted a children's playground on the same site since the 1940s, as well as being the one-time hunting ground of Henry VIII. Unsurprisingly, the Royal Parks didn't opt for a Tudor theme when revamping the equipment, instead drawing on the area's maritime connections with a vast sand- and water-play area and a smattering of boat-like structures. Accessibility is a major consideration of the playground's design, as is a focus on collaborative play, with abundant opportunities for kids to work together as a crew. Plenty more nautical fun awaits at the neighbouring National Maritime Museum's Ahoy! indoor play zone.

SE10 8XG
Nearest station: Maze Hill
Facilities: Toilets, baby change, cafe, picnic benches

SOUTH

41

BATTERSEA PARK PLAYGROUND

Expansive play paradise for all ages

It's rare to find a playground so gargantuan that kids don't know where to begin, but it's a problem often encountered at Battersea Park's sprawling play metropolis. Technically several play areas clustered together, the site comprises a toddler zone with ride-on vehicles; a more demanding juniors' area with a colourful slide tower; and a physically (and, at times, emotionally) challenging over-8s section whose structures are almost as lofty as the Go Ape treetop walkways that encircle it. The park's children's zoo and pedalo-stocked lake make a good case for staying all day, though Chelsea's iconic Saatchi Gallery and the National Army Museum's themed play space are well worth the walk across the river.

SW11 4NJ

Nearest station: Battersea Park

Facilities: Toilets, baby change, cafe, picnic benches

42
CATOR PARK NORTH PLAYGROUND

Ambitious play space for courageous kids

Nestled among the foliage of Cator Park, a biodiverse green space established as part of the new Kidbrooke Village, this epic playscape may originally have been intended to serve the young residents, but its appeal extends far beyond the estate's boundary thanks to its wildly inventive design. Looping tunnel slides sprout from four-sided, branch-topped nests, making them resemble kites when viewed from above and earning the spot the nickname 'Kite Park'. They're just one part of this incredible space, which also hosts a bouldering wall, hillside slides, bridges and balance beams, along with dozens of climbing opportunities – and even more at neighbouring Sutcliffe Park Sports Centre's all-weather Clip 'n' Climb.

Kidbrooke Park Road, SE3 9FY
Nearest station: Kidbrooke

SOUTH

43
THE MAGIC GARDEN, HAMPTON COURT PALACE

Enchanting playground on historic site

Magic comes alive at this bewitching playground, even if its mythical beasts have seemingly been turned to stone by a malevolent king. Speaking of which, entry is included when you buy a ticket to Henry VIII's most famous residence, but won't be granted without one – so be sure to set aside a couple of hours to do it justice. A game of hide and seek should quickly acquaint kids with this enchanting space, which incorporates treetop walks, stately towers, concealed lairs, a king-sized water-play area and a gargantuan ruby-eyed dragon. Adults, meanwhile, should start at the on-site kiosk, where they can grab coffee and cake before taking a pew and watching the fairytale fun unfold.

KT8 9AU
Nearest station: Hampton Court
Facilities: Toilets, baby change, cafe, picnic benches

44
PROSPECT PLACE PLAYGROUND

Vibrant playscape in power station development

It might stand in the vast shadow of Battersea's iconic power station, but this shiny playground is no shrinking violet. In fact, violet is just one of the many colours in its kaleidoscopic palette. Built around a quartet of play towers – from which rope bridges, twisting tube slides and spiral staircases shoot – this eye-popping playscape packs a powerful punch in spite of its modest footprint, providing hours of playtime in an exceptionally striking package. Balance equipment, bucket swings and a tilting roundabout complete the offer, while the undulating rainbow hillscape provides endless scope for floor-is-lava-style shenanigans. Worked up an appetite? Refuel at kid-friendly spots such as Megan's, Tonkotsu or Where the Pancakes Are.

Circus Road West, SW8 5BN
Nearest station: Battersea Power Station
Facilities: Toilets, baby change, cafe, picnic benches

SOUTH

45
CANONS PLAYGROUND

Topsy-turvy timber playscape

It's no surprise that this creative playground was co-designed by children. Located in the grounds of the historic Canons House – and next to a rather less historic leisure centre – this stimulating space draws inspiration from the site's medieval dovecot, with two of its structures reimagining the building as a series of multi-use dens. Elsewhere, an ingenious mountain of timber folds takes its cues from the kids' experiments with scrunched-up paper, and can be clambered on or crawled beneath, while tilted forms create the illusion of a dizzying parallel universe where everything is delightfully off-kilter. Pop into the leisure centre for more high-octane fun in the form of soft play and Aqua Splash inflatable assault-course sessions.

Canons Leisure Centre, Madeira Road, CR4 4HD
Nearest station: Mitcham Junction
Facilities: Toilets, baby change, cafe, picnic benches

46
PECKHAM RYE PLAYGROUND

Tumbling streams and towering structures

Whether they're two or ten, kids are sure to find their thing at this bold and beautiful playground. Located in the centre of Peckham Rye Park and Common, this spacious site is dominated by an impressive water-play landscape featuring cascading streams, retractable dams and easy-to-activate water pumps, as well as a spectacular, if rather unnerving, arrangement of wooden stilts, wobbly bridges and near-vertical slides for the park's longer-limbed visitors. Plentiful swings and a series of sand-dipped wooden playhouses equipped with compact slides seal the deal, while ample adult seating and proximity to the park cafe ensure it's an all-day affair.

Peckham Rye Common, SE15 3UA
Nearest station: Nunhead
Facilities: Toilets, baby change, cafe, picnic benches

SOUTH

47
BROCKWELL PARK PLAYGROUND

Water, wood and miniature train rides

Wood seems to be the overarching theme of Brockwell Park's sprawling playscape, and while that might not sound particularly unique or adventurous, it somehow accomplishes both. A proper destination playground, it offers a broad appeal across age groups, with small playhouses, larger forts and huge log hangouts creating a village-like design that inspires collaborative play across the entire space. Sizzling days call for an invigorating splash in the park's wet-play area – a heaven-sent combination of a rocky splash pond and capacious paddling pool. On the other side of the park, the miniature railway tootles between Herne Hill Gate (close to children's bookshop The Paper Cat) and Brockwell Lido on Sundays from March to October.

Brockwell Park Gardens, SE24 0NG
Nearest station: Herne Hill
Facilities: Toilets, baby change, cafe, picnic benches

48
DEXTERS ADVENTURE PLAYGROUND

Timber fun house on a significant site

Though sparse in terms of its loose parts, this modest plot is home to one of the most breathtaking fixed structures we've found in an adventure playground. Drawing inspiration from houses on the street that were destroyed in the Brixton Riots, this glorious tangle of wood features playable domestic elements, including sloped planks that mimic bannisters, drainpipe ladders to scale and cosy attic spaces that look out across the neighbourhood. On Saturdays, kids of all ages are invited to explore the playground, while a youth club for teens and pre-teens runs after school and in the holidays. Head down via Koala Coffee for pre-play lattes (or post-play ice creams).

6 Montego Close, SE24 0LH
Nearest station: Brixton
Facilities: Toilets

SOUTH

49
CLAPHAM PARK ESTATE PLAYGROUND

50-year-old Brutalist folly

London's oldest-surviving play structure still packs a punch more than half a century after it was produced – thanks to some clever engineering and a solid commitment to maintenance. Built in 1969, this Brutalist creation might at first seem uninspiring, with its grey concrete shell and stark spiral form, but it's this nonprescriptive design that makes it so appealing – and probably one of the reasons why it's survived this long. The gently sloped, meandering slide is as fun to scramble up as it is to slither down, while its tunnels make excellent dens and the tiled dome begs to be scaled. Speaking of which, nearby climbing centre Substation's kids' room is a dream come true for budding boulderers.

Belgravia House, Clarence Avenue, SW4 8HY
Nearest station: Clapham South

SOUTH

50
VICTORY COMMUNITY PARK

Striking playground in hidden-gem park

Once an underused mishmash of garishly painted metal, this tucked-away park emerged victorious from a handsome redesign in early 2025. Established by local residents in the 1980s, the little-known green space feels quieter and more personal than the adjoining Elephant Park, while enjoying easy access to its plethora of restaurants and popular Elephant Springs (no.38) splash pad. Fabricated with plenty of natural timber to tune in with the leafy surrounds, the eye-catching playground boasts a large ball court and lofty climbing structure for older kids and teens, along with smaller, matching constructions for under-5s. When the sun goes in, proceed to Four Quarters for hot dogs and Donkey Kong, or Four Hundred Rabbits for kid-pleasing pizzas.

Victory Place, SE17 1PG
Nearest station: Elephant & Castle
Facilities: Picnic benches

SOUTH

51
ANNE KEANE PLAYGROUND

Landscaped utopia named after local campaigner

Situated halfway between Borough and Elephant and Castle, next to the estate that once housed its namesake – local campaigner Anne, who was the driving force behind the park development – this bumpy beauty is excellent for all ages. Apparatus is suited to toddlers up to tweens, elegantly arranged across a spongy green, yellow and violet hillscape. For younger kids, there's an accessible roundabout, baby swings, static wooden climb-on animals and an endearing elephant slide while more seasoned adventurers can wrestle with wobbly hillside bridges, a rough ride of a slide, and a tangle of logs built for serious scrambling. Spend around an hour here, then head to Bad Moon Cafe for board games and pizzas, or to the Imperial War Museum for a hands-on history lesson.

Dickens Fields, 10 Dickens Square, SE1 4JL
Nearest stations: Borough, Elephant & Castle

52
BRUNEL ESTATE

One of the last surviving 1970s slides

Not many playgrounds can lay claim to a Grade II-listed slide, but then not many slides make it into their fifth (nearly sixth) decade. Laid out during the construction of Westbourne Park's Brunel Estate in 1973, this modernist masterpiece consists of a long sliver of metal cascading through a colossal, bespoke climbing structure made entirely from red brick. The equipment that sits alongside the large slide is pretty standard issue, so once you're done bolting down this beauty, make a beeline for Museum of Brands' nostalgic Time Tunnel or the revered ramps and rails of BAYSIXTY6 skate park.

Westbourne Park Road, W2 5UZ
Nearest stations: Westbourne Park, Royal Oak

53
THE CHILDREN'S GARDEN, KEW GARDENS

Plant-themed playground at World Heritage site

'What do plants need to grow?' ponder the stepping stones that line the path leading to this awe-inspiring space. Kids needn't look far to find the answers – they're right there in the form of four distinct play zones, each one themed around the needs in question. The Earth Zone is all about worming through slides and digging in the sand, while the Air Zone will appeal to smaller ones with its 'pollen' spheres and trampolines. The Water Zone is a maze of paddling ponds and rockpools, while the Sun Zone functions as a chillout space with its large lawn and glowing sun tunnel. Peckish post-play? Head to the Family Kitchen for stone-baked pizza and eye-popping ice cream.

TW9 3AE
Nearest station: Kew Gardens
Facilities: Toilets, baby change, cafe, picnic benches

54
PADDINGTON RECREATION GROUND

Showstopping space with literary theme

Paddington Bear references abound at what is arguably the capital's most inventive play space, despite most being so subtle you'll likely miss them (and the fact that this isn't technically Paddington). A row of pastel-hued townhouses recalls the Brown family's fictional Windsor Gardens home and conceals a vertical wooden maze, while the adorable railway station and play train reference their charge's arrival in London. Elsewhere, a stunner of a steamboat alludes to Paddington's voyage to England from darkest Peru, linking up to a bridge that connects the playground's two halves. Once you've explored both, wander south to Little Venice and the Puppet Barge Theatre, whose magical marionette performances are a particular hit with families.

Randolph Avenue, W9 1PF
Nearest station: Maida Vale
Facilities: Toilets, baby change, cafe, picnic benches

55
HOBBLEDOWN HEATH

Steampunk-style kids' metropolis

This Hobbiton-esque amusement park packs in so many play structures, it's borderline ridiculous – though at least the substantial admission fee is (just about) justified. Particularly well suited to older kids, Hobbledown's second instalment is more than twice the size of its Epsom sister-site, offering four thrilling fantasy play areas designed to pique their imaginations, test their scrambling skills and fuel some serious fun. Each play 'village' has its own unique character, from the madcap Cribble Creek, with its twisting chutes, slides and wheels, to the bustling Buckbridge Market with its role-play-ready shops. Add in aerial adventures, an epic indoor Play Barn and an on-site zoo, and it might be worth investing in annual membership.

Staines Road, TW14 0HH
Nearest stations: Feltham, Hounslow West
Facilities: Toilets, baby change, cafe, picnic benches

56

HOLLAND PARK ADVENTURE PLAYGROUND

Inspiring play in striking setting

Is it any coincidence that possibly the capital's best-looking park contains what is likely its best-looking playground? And, far from being just a pretty face, it offers what might be its most exciting play experience, too. This gorgeously landscaped, imaginatively designed wonderland allows kids of all ages and abilities to push their physical boundaries, whether they're scaling the soaring Fishing Tower's network of ropes, navigating the swirling Hillcoaster's sloping walkway or braving what might be the most forceful zip wire we've ever encountered. Speaking of great design, the iconic Design Museum is right on the doorstep, while kids' boutiques Hop Like a Bunny and Mini Rodini are great for gifts.

55 Abbotsbury Road, W14 8EL
Nearest stations: Holland Park, Kensington (Olympia)
Facilities: Toilets, baby change, cafe, picnic benches

57
WHITFIELD GARDENS PLAY AREA

Challenging play in central setting

Despite sitting in the shadow of one of London's most easily recognisable buildings (yep, the big BT tower), remarkably few people seem to be aware of this clandestine playground's existence. Closed on term-time weekdays, the space is best suited to 8–12s, who are welcome to swing by on weekends and holidays to sample its delights. Apparatus is on the scarce side, with a towering treehouse and expansive climbing wall making up the bulk of the offer, but the playground is unique in providing space for children to safely indulge in risky play in the heart of the city. Combine one of the area's many museums, be it the British, Grant or Foundling.

54a Whitfield Street, W1T 4ER
Nearest station: Goodge Street

58

DIANA MEMORIAL PLAYGROUND

Finding Neverland in Kensington

If you only visit one London playground, this Peter Pan-themed paradise should probably be it. Dedicated to the late Princess of Wales, this sandy playscape feels every inch the otherworldly wonderland with its exotic trees, remarkably realistic Jolly Roger and an outer wall that serves to block out the surrounding landscape, creating a truly immersive environment in which to lose yourself (and not your child). And while the aforementioned Jolly Roger might be the star of the show, the fun definitely doesn't stop there, with summer-ready sand and water play, Lost Boys-inspired treehouses and loads more to explore around the 'island' – as well as the Diana Memorial play fountain just beyond.

Kensington Gardens, Broad Walk, W2 4RU
Nearest station: Queensway
Facilities: Toilets, baby change, cafe, picnic benches

WEST

59
NORTHALA FIELDS PLAYGROUND

Quirky construction in unique park

It might sound (and look) like something out of *The Chronicles of Narnia*, but this fantasy playscape can be found just off the A40 (and not at the back of a wardrobe). Located at the foot of the park's four artificial mounds, which were magicked from the rubble of the old Wembley Stadium, the playground takes the form of a single, sprawling playframe constructed almost entirely from golden timber logs. Different levels cater to different age groups and are connected by a labyrinthine network of ladders and bridges of varying levels of precariousness. Once they've exhausted that (and themselves), head to Hanwell Zoo in search of miniature donkeys, lemurs, margays and capybaras.

Westway Close, UB5 6UR
Nearest station: Northolt
Facilities: Toilets, cafe, picnic benches

IMAGE CREDITS

P.2 © Martin Usborne; p.4 © Martin Usborne; p.5 © RAF Museum; p.6 © Duncan & Grove; p.7 © Discover Children's Story Centre / Sorcha Bridge; p.8 © Martin Usborne; Three Corners © Martin Usborne; Alf Barrett © Ann Waldvogel; Golden Lane Estate © Taran Wilkhu; Spa Fields © Martin Usborne; Coram's Fields © Martin Usborne; Stationers Park © Ann Waldvogel; Alexandra Road Park © Ann Waldvogel; Gloucester Gate © Martin Usborne; Royal Air Force Museum © RAF Museum; Kilburn Grange Park © Ann Waldvogel; Marylebone Green © PA Images / Alamy Stock Photo; Claremont Park © Duncan & Grove; Highgate Wood © Martin Usborne; Astey's Row © Martin Usborne; Spring Park © Martin Usborne; Highbury Fields © Martin Usborne; Barnard Adventure Playground © Ann Waldvogel; Hornsey Park © Ann Waldvogel; Somerford Grove © Emmy Watts; Queen's Park © Ann Waldvogel; St Jude Street Garden © Ann Waldvogel; Hoppa Play and Skate Park © HTA Design, development by Vistry and Enfield Council, play park landcaping by PFL, landscape architecture by HTA Design; Parsloes Park ©Thierry Bal; West Ham Park © Martin Usborne; Biodiversity Playground © Martin Usborne; Sunrise Close © Martin Usborne; Harbour Quay Wood Wharf Play Space, Marvellous Maze, Play Design: Erect Archiecture, Photography: Henrietta Williams; All Mead Gardens © Martin Usborne; Forrester Way Play Area © Duncan & Grove; Barking Park first image © Ann Waldvogel, second image © Robin Forster Photography / LDA Design; Tumbling Bay first image Tumbling Bay Architecture & Play Design: Erect Architecture, Photography: David Grandorge, second and third images © Martin Usborne; Victoria Park © Martin Usborne; Stonebridge Gardens © Ann Waldvogel; Hackney Downs © Emmy Watts; Discover Children's Story Centre © Discover Children's Story Centre / Sorcha Bridge; Brunswick Park © Ann Waldvogel Burgess Park Woodland Playground © Duncan & Grove; Elephant Springs © John Sturrock / Gillespies; Jubilee Gardens © Martin Usborne; Greenwich Park © The Royal Parks; Battersea Park © Martin Usborne; Cator Park North © Simon Winson / Berkeley Group; The Magic Garden, Hampton Court Palace first image © Martin Usborne, second image © Historic Royal Palaces / David Hedges, third image © Martin Usborne; Prospect Place © Ann Waldvogel; Canons Playground © Studio Hardie; Peckham Rye Playground © Ann Waldvogel; Brockwell Park © Ann Waldvogel; Dexters Adventure Playground © Dellali Defor, Bigkid Foundation; Clapham Park Estate © Emmy Watts; Victory Community Park © Emmy Watts; Anne Keane Playground © Ann Waldvogel; Brunel Estate © Jack Young; The Children's Garden, Kew Gardens first image by Charlie J Ercilla / Alamy Stock Photo, second image © Martin Usborne, third image © Duncan & Grove; Paddington Recreation Ground © Martin Usborne; Hobbledown Heath © Paul Taylor; Holland Park Adventure Playground, Landscape & Play Design: Erect Architecture, Photography: Henrietta Williams; Whitfield Gardens © Martin Usborne; Diana Memorial Playground first image © Peter Phipp/Travelshots.com / Alamy Stock Photo, second image © Martin Usborne; Northala Fields first image © The Children's Playground, second image @markoandplacemakers

An Opinionated Guide to London Playgrounds
First edition, first printing

Published in 2025 by Hoxton Mini Press, London
Copyright © Hoxton Mini Press 2025. All rights reserved.

Text by Emmy Watts
Editing by Kate Overy
Production design by Dom Grant
Production control by David Brimble
Proofreading by Florence Ward
Editorial support by Flora MacKenzie
and Richard Enright

With thanks to Matthew Young for
initial series design.

Some of the images and text in this book
originally appeared in an earlier version,
London's Best Playgrounds (2023).

Please note: we recommend checking the
websites listed for each entry before you
visit for the latest information on price,
opening times and pre-booking
requirements.

The right of Emmy Watts to be identified
as the creator of this Work has been
asserted under the Copyright, Designs and
Patents Act 1988.

Thank you to all of the individuals and
institutions who have provided images
and arranged permissions. While every
effort has been made to trace the present
copyright holders we apologise in advance
for any unintentional omission or error,
and would be pleased to insert the
appropriate acknowledgement in any
subsequent edition.

No part of this publication may be
reproduced, stored in a retrieval system,
or transmitted in any form or by any
means, electronic, mechanical,
photocopying, recording or otherwise,
without the prior written permission of
the copyright owner.

A CIP catalogue record for this book is
available from the British Library.

ISBN: 978-1-917719-07-0

Printed and bound by OZGraf, Poland

Manufacturer: Hoxton Mini Press, 104
Northside Studios, 16–29 Andrews Road,
London E8 4QF, UK
www.hoxtonminipress.com

Represented by: Authorised Rep
Compliance Ltd., Ground Floor, 71 Lower
Baggot Street, Dublin D02 P593, Ireland
www.arccompliance.com

Hoxton Mini Press is an environmen-
tally conscious publisher, committed
to offsetting our carbon footprint.
This book is 100 per cent carbon
compensated, with offset purchased
from Stand For Trees.

Every time you order from our website, we
plant a tree: www.hoxtonminipress.com

Selected opinionated guides in the series:

 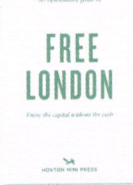  

For more go to www.hoxtonminipress.com

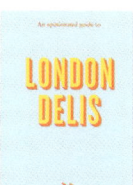

INDEX

Alexandra Road Park, *7*
Alf Barrett Playground, *2*
All Mead Gardens, *28*
Anne Keane Playground, *51*
Astey's Row Playground, *14*
Barking Park Playground, *30*
Barnard Adventure Playground, *17*
Battersea Park Playground, *41*
Biodiversity Playground, *25*
Brockwell Park Playground, *47*
Brunel Estate, *52*
Brunswick Park Playground, *36*
Burgess Park Woodland Playground, *37*
Canons Playground, *45*
Cator Park North Playground, *42*
The Children's Garden, Kew Gardens, *53*
Clapham Park Estate Playground, *49*
Claremont Park Playground, *12*
Coram's Fields, *5*
Dexters Adventure Playground, *48*
Diana Memorial Playground, *58*
Discover Children's Story Centre, *35*
Elephant Springs, *38*
Forrester Way Play Area, *29*
Gloucester Gate Playground, *8*
Golden Lane Estate Play Space, *3*
Greenwich Park Playground, *40*
Hackney Downs Playground, *34*
Harbour Quay Maze Play Area, *27*
Highbury Fields Playground, *16*
Highgate Wood Playground, *13*
Hobbledown Heath, *55*
Holland Park Adventure Playground, *56*
Hoppa Play and Skate Park, *22*
Hornsey Park Playground, *18*
Jubilee Gardens Playground, *39*
Kilburn Grange Park Play Area, *10*
The Magic Garden, Hampton Court Palace, *43*
Marylebone Green Playground, *11*
Northala Fields Playground, *59*
Paddington Recreation Ground, *54*
Parsloes Park, *23*
Peckham Rye Playground, *46*
Prospect Place Playground, *44*
Queen's Park Playground, *20*
Royal Air Force Museum Playground, *9*
Somerford Grove Playground, *19*
Spa Fields Playground, *4*
Spring Park Playground, *15*
St Jude Street Garden, *21*
Stationers Park, *6*
Stonebridge Gardens, *33*
Sunrise Close Play Area, *26*
Three Corners Adventure Playground, *1*
Tumbling Bay Playground, *31*
Victoria Park Playgrounds, *32*
Victory Community Park, *50*
West Ham Park Playground, *24*
Whitfield Gardens Play Area, *57*